Catch the Moment

A Collection of Narrative Poetry

By Patrick D. Kaiser

Contents

Memento – Mori

Irrefutable

Empty Quiver

Me

Dream on

Midnight stroll

The stage

Contents - cont'd

Monotone

Phoenix

Reality setting in

Distance

A ballad of fallen angels

Paper Memories

The House on Poppy Hill

For all those who've supported me up to
this point

when all hope seemed lost.

Without you I would not be here.

Abstract Poems

Unto the river

What comes before the calming storm

Than chaos – Unfiltered, unfettered noise

Day by day, night after unrelenting night

I am only clear unto myself

For the ones - Them & they

Cannot understand,

Or is it won't?

Impossible to decipher

Improbable to me

The wayward run

Here & there

There abouts – Everywhere

The cogs in my head
A confusing mess of oil and grease
To them perplexed
If only I would – If only I could
Convey them – My internal mechanisms

Perhaps then?
Perhaps not?
Stumbling – Stumbling
Words in which I'm caught
Easier?
Yes, & as the years gone by
Still – still a struggle
As a cast die

Note: This poem conveys the struggle

Of myself and many others

With autism.

Brave Blue

Marching along, I hear the ticking

Tick tock – Tick tock

Ever present, the pace quickening

Tick tock – Tick tock

The hands of life, counting down

Blue water flowing – What a sound

Surrounded by events that devour hope

Tick tock – Tick tock

Among the world, devastation glows

For what reason need I give it power?

As, here, birds sing upon the hour

a sky, blue, smiling at me

As white cloud pass

That's all I see

Here it grows from the ground

Petals, blue – It's beauty astounds

It blossoms in a way that few can know

A way that reaps what is sewn

Here, on this mountain – Away from it all

Peace envelopes – Mind, body & soul

Nature thrives in the void

"What could destroy this?" I ask you to say

What force may take this beauty, heavenly
made?

These hills of stone in the rolling distance

This symbiotic place – One of eternal consistence

Beyond the reach of chaos and war

I think I'll remain a while more

The many colors – The shades, the hues

It's beauty brave – A brave blue

Human

Time passes

The pendulum sways

What then?

Who are we to be called human?

The dark – The light

It swallows us whole

A contradicting energy

A conflicting typhoon

Churning against itself

That we might be called worthy

Of something greater than ourselves

Greater than our world

Greater than our sky

Greater than our destiny

Yet, we, as human amount to dust

Born from the earth

Ending – Returning to it

Only our legacy

Our history

We take nothing

What we leave behind

That is what makes us

Human

Love

What is life?

What are we?

To claim, so sweet, our loved ones

Those who bear with us

Those who call us friend

The ones, to whom, our existence is
acknowledged

Even when the dark breaks us

They ever remain, unwavering, by our side

It matters not what we can't r don't have

It matters only – Acknowledging those
who remain

They who acknowledge us

For life is love

Given – Not received

Even when we feel the dark

The loneliness – The sorrow – The guilt

Our anger – Amounting to nothing, but
poison

Died by the light in our lives

Light is love

Love is life

A declaration of war

A dark abyss swallows my soul

Lonely – Cold – Out of control

I push & I push

Inside, always breaking

Never forgetting – Never forsaking

A smile, simple, hiding my fear

As the struggle rages

Holding back my tears

Strength? - Weakness?

That I carry on

Making them smile – Trying t least

Strength? - Weakness?

I have not taken that release

I refuse to lose

Unto my shadow

I can't stop fighting

I don't know how

I'll keep him at bay

Continue to smile

Relying on friends & faith all the while

Sorrow unending

Pain is nothing

That's just life

It's always something

And so, here, I make this declaration of war

Keep is coming

More & more

Day breaks bell

The chilling night devours me

To the point of nightmares seen

Into the precipice thus I go

down the rabbit hole of my fears

Falling – Falling

Until day breaks glow

One to the next

As real they seem

One to the next

A dream of a dream

Psychedelic here – Complacent there

A riddle waking: Do I dare?

A soothing comfort to remain

Or facing reality – Be driven insane

And that – The conundrum

So very hard to choose

Mental in dreams – Mental in life

As if a trapeze artist

Upon the edge of a knife

In the caress of slumber, having all I desire

Yet, in waking, Satisfaction comes with a
blazing fire

To earn my claims – Enveloping –
Cathartic

Why give that up to the illusion karmic?

I feel it now – Breaking free

The warming light of morn, it streams

The tone echoes in my ear

Contentment, coursing through my veins

Letting go the falsehood, that in sleep,
chains

Down my cheek it thus flows

This honest tear – Freeing me from hell

As dawn dances by day breaks bell

Memento – Mori

And so, the tale is told

No bias to the young – No bias to the old

Life, simple or so it seems

Ending in a flash with sparkling gleam

Take heed... & know this

No stigma to bear – Deaths kiss

We reap what we sew

In this garden we lay

What blooms then, we plant today

No luggage to pack

When that day comes

All we lack – Ensnared

The beat of the drum

What is left to their memories – Their hearts?

Residing on this earth after we've gone

What semblance remains of our mark?

Heed this tale from Latin old

A ever destined, to each of us, told

Let it be a warning in all its glory

This, the story of Memento - Mori

Irrefutable

Logical: what one may call

Gravity...

Of it's purest nature

Powerfully brief

Thus what we may

Other evidences of science

Arithmetic – Factual

No equal to ever compare

Language – Solidified

It's ever compounding laws

The art of emotion

Even they, compelled by logic

Anger – Sadness – Joy

A cause they possess

The one elusive science

May we call it art

One that holds such might

Over we – Feeble humans

What is this "love" that we feel?

Love that compels us

To throw all caution to the wind

Love that we die for

Love that we pursue

Such reckless abandonment

Love by its nature

Cannot pair with logic

Yet love

We allow no quarter – No bias

A power – Unimaginable

A gift – Irrefutable

It is

Empty quiver

Rustling, rustling – Feather soft

Sound breaking, you fly aloft

From release to mark

Straight & true

Soaring high – These memories of you

Waiting – Waking

The edge – The point

Until the moment the whistle stops

All the luck of a flipping coin

Until the moment... it drops

Oh, excitement & anticipation

Resounding, the world – More than a nation

Down to the last of oaken shaft

Through the night – Brightly burning

Into flame – Into ash

Striking now, straw & wood

This final shot – All that's good

Visibly, this shot remains

Ever fearless & Ever Plain

A true archer you have been

As an empty quiver – Now free

<u>ME</u>

Does anyone hear me?

Or are my words simply vacant?

As the sand falls grain by grain

I wonder...

Through it all

Falling – Falling

Through the void

I pass my selves

The mes of today, yesterday & tomorrow

They speak, only unto their own ears

A dreadful place to find

Through it all

Madness, unfolding

To which do I convey?

Original? - Copies?

The lonesome & the broken

Falling – Falling

To each their own

The longing of self

The loss of the whole

Broken thus...

Madness...

Insanity...

Starving of truth...

What now?

What to give?

What to do?

That the cycle might end

No answers unto me

Given nor received

Arrived nor left

On & on – No end

The spinning hands

Dizzying, yet void

Null of any justification

Time, fickle

That we might make it our own

It bows to none

Answering only unto reality

A bashful, confident loop

For eternity

<u>Dream on</u>

Wake up in the morning

Just keep snoring

Your dream is just that good

Get better? It could

You want to know what happens next?

Your heart may beat straight out of your chest

that, my friend, is the one true test

In dreams

Loosing touch with reality

Putting faith in fantasies

All that I can say

Is that it's ok

Dream, dream your life away

I said dream

Dream on

Dream down to your core

Dream – Dream & dream some more

<u>Midnight stroll</u>

What is mortality?

Is it illogical?

Is it a fallacy

Perhaps – Plausible

What makes us human?

Is it our genes?

A noose for a hangman

upon a tree

The red bloom of a rose

May I propose?

A theory far fetched

All alone – No reason to bet

The moon in the sky, shaped of a nail

our faces in awe – Inspired never to fail

Mortality...

Such a triviality

Illogical

To the point of methodical

If we, for a turn, went astray

Would you call for me on that day?

Fallacies

More triviality

Monotonic

Will we never be fixed?

Plausible

To make a turn for the worse

As I stumble

Over ever word

Mortality

Simply that

Nothing more

Sit on back

Enjoy this show

I, walking down the road

Neither the darkness not the light

Down the middle to the dawn of twilight

The stage

To the roar of applause I tread

For my inspiration – You

For their memory, them & they

The ones who push me

They push me

To that place beyond myself

Limits, no more

That I might reach their hearts

Who then am I to them?

Racing down this path

At the finish

That I might find myself here

Waiting only to feel

To let myself free

The flood gates open

My tears burst forth

Me, simple & clear

That this light might be mine

This place the overture

That place, My curtain call

Past - Present - Future

A standing ovation

Into peace I step

A light – My legacy

Inspiration unto the next

This alone

I dream

Narrative Poems

Grace – Too late

Frozen hands on the face

Echoing – Echoing

Killing me without a trace

The silence loud in my ear

What then, oh my – Oh dear, oh dear

That's it – I'm done

Life, not worth living

Without her there's no chance

Mistaken-mistakes, unforgiving

Time stops, here, in this place

The gavel drops in empty space

There's only one authority I can recognize

As I've been setup by both our lies

I'm guilty – I'm guilty of a lot of things

But murder?

That's not one I bring

Upon you, myself or my families wings

Oh my - Oh my - What then

If grace, there is, such a thing

I plead for it

"Oh please, oh please

Do not condemn me for this crime

This crime, alone, which is not mine."

"Guilty!" The jury rings out

And the hands start moving around &
around

In this instance time moves quicker than
quick

As it sears like the wax of a candle stick

"But I'm innocent!"

I beg & I plead

As they drag me,

My shackles at my knees

Years pass – Time flows

Twenty seven years, so it goes

As I step out, feet touch the ground

I long, only, for the bars around

I plead for grace

It never came

Now, it comes as pain remains

Grace – Too late

A day, a day

The boots

The last remnants, covered in soot

The leather, scarred and worn

They stand, ever still…

Watchful - My shield from the kill

To see them in action

How I wish it could've been

For the man whose souls did fill

These boots stained by blood

Perched upon the hill

An ivory tower carved in stone

The name engraved in thee

So many more to remember

The boots symbolic of he

They trekked through the mud,

The blood & the muck

Yet still they marched on through

No doubt, no remorse, and no retreat to see

They bore every guilt to protect me and
you

And even now, as they stand empty

They forever weather the storm

Evcr vigilant, ever strong

Ever a soldier, the norm

<u>Noise</u>

Oh how I could certainly tell

The wildest of tales

Of attempts tried

And those that failed

Of the screech…

Of the song,

Of the melody thus

What came next

Of ambition and lust

A tingling, a tickle in my ear

To the high note,

To the low…

To the very last

How I crumbled, the memory haunting

How I'm humbled at the sound of nothing

A staunch shock as fear took hold

Noise…

Then nothing, but the shivering cold

No note, ever to reach me again

Only the colors and how they blend

What I'm left with,

A lingering will

Nothing ever as hard to swallow

My pride, dissolved like a pill

Let this be a lesson to you

Karma is real and it rings true

A noise, left…

A noise, forgot

If only, if only,

But it's not…

<u>Forgot</u>

Oh simple, the sight

Of my last right

It's the straw, breaking my back

My heart fading to black

These simple things,

They drive me mad

To the point,

The single point

All that's seen is the bad

The height of my feet

The weight of the fall

Who then am I to them all?

Inside I know, even in this low

I'm a son,

I'm a friend

I'm the one keeping them

From this exact end

What am I doing here,

But losing to myself,

To the dark, a shattered glass on a shelf

Thinking it now,

Am I really so selfish?

That I'd break them down

Simply for a point,

Recognition, mine

Though not quite how it goes

What happens when this hit's their ears?

What good does it bring?

Only sadness and tears

This is not me,

A villain I am not,

To put those who love me

Into the file: forgot

World's end

Turning, turning

All for not

What remains?

What's forgot?

Every good thing

Must come to an end

Same for us

& same for them

Fire rains from the sky

But for this…

I can not cry

"Will you stay with me

Until the end?

Until the moment our lives blend?"

You give a smile

That's all I need

Now, in peace

I can bleed…

Resting here, in your arms

Keeping me safe from harm

Every other, the times I've left

But in the end, only you, bereft

It matters not, anyone else

In the end, I blame myself

But you, here, with me now

I find myself watching the clouds

It's almost over, the end, here

I just wish to make one thing clear

I'm content, ending this way

You and me, here we lay

Kissing my face, you & the wind

I can finally smile at the world's end

Phantom understanding

In a moment

She's there

In a moment

She's gone

I don't understand it

As my sanity is bursting at the seams

The question…

It wanes

"Who is she?"

Why, oh why do I see?

Reality

A mind melding opponent

It toys with me

Playing its game

It will not win

I will stay sane

A trick of the light?

Perhaps…

Or,

A flicker of shadow

Against candles

Against glass

I see her everywhere

More and more

It makes me dizzy

My head throbs sore

She startles me

When I'm in school…

And When I'm not

She startles me at home

"WHAT?!

WHAT?!

What is it?

What does she want with me?"

I have to know

What does she want with me?

Just let me go?

Today is normal, at least at start

But who knows?

The finish may break my heart

My name is Jason, Jason Green

Today it's revealed

What all it means

Monotone

A taken picture, attempted, failed

Called but a dream

What then comes of it…

After the fact?

My focus, my heart, perhaps the subject

My dark room, my only solace

As dozens of times I've tried

Birthed a masterpiece

One to never be named

If only I could do it justice,

This monotone imitation, nothing but an insult

The colors I saw, the beauty, the stone

The water so crisp, as it, drawn to the clouds,

Heavenly fair,

What was that place?

The one I saw…

Above the clouds…

A floating city, lost to age

Yet still,

She, there, as a bird, caged

Alone there, in the tallest tower of ivory stone

The last remnant, captured thus in
monotone

To find again what took me years

Would take yet all I have

More than worth it's weight in gold

To set foot upon that ivory stone

Just a name, that's all I ask

As all that is left from that flash

Ivory stone, and water crisp

Monotone, a name?

Indeed, but from her lips

Phoenix

Ash like snow

Kissing my skin, It falls

The bitter warmth of the flame

The crack of the light, it dances

Sirens in the distance announces their presence

"Help" is what they're called

Yet where were they when it all came crashing down?

Left to the dust, those, without hope

The ringing echoes in my skull

The tactile splinter, the match

Rolls between the two,

My digits, callused and worn

With this, I've nothing to return to

And my hope residing, like the wind

It carries me, a new life, a new story

My progressing thought, shivering with the
cold

One of my own making

This match, the pen

This place, parchment, fresh & blank

Finally, I'm free

Free unto the flame

As the billowing smoke,

The smell of ash

Releases me

From my past

Reality setting in

Steps away from death

Minutes away from the end

As here I stand at my crossroads

Everything I thought I knew

"Kill or be killed?"

The words

The taste of poison off my tongue

To save a life?

Even her life?

Is it worth it?

I don't want her to die,

"But… to kill him…"

Would break it apart

My already broken mind

It's pushing me to the brink

I'm so conflicted

I'm so confused

As doubt takes hold

"Will I fail?"

The question

"Fail to save all at stake?"

Blood rushes, and pressure builds

"All that's come to matter?"

Behind my eyes I'm cracking

"If another life lost…

One so close

I couldn't do it;

Continue,

Go on."

"Go on,

DO IT!"

His voice echoes cold to the bone

"IF YOU CAN!

...Or I will."

It's clear - he means it

Someone has to die

I feel my heart

It tears itself asunder

I didn't even consider this

Not even a flicker

Across the plain of my mind

I was idealistic

Prideful

And now I just don't know

"What will happen?"

The question

The deepest question…

Has yet an answer

For all my trying,

This is how it ends?

I was foolish

I was arrogant

I am a fool, crowned king

Nothing less

Nothing more

My decision?

I don't know!

I'm pathetic…

It's all pathetic…

Like glass it all shatters

And secrets scatter to the wind

Carrying us to the end

Pathetic!

PATHETIC!!!!!!

He raises it

Cocking it back

Gleaming black of metal

Finger on the trigger

"Last chance, hero."

His voice as burning venom

Pointing it… at her

I'm grateful for the small fact

That she's unconscious

I hear it as loud as thunder

The click

My decision…

Is…

As reality sets

The gun sounds

"BANG!!!"

Distance

The earth turns and time fades

When I can see your smile,

This crystal saline, rolling down my cheek

When I can use that word

"Love"

That's distance

Now that I'm strong, and our place is now

This world, cold, turns upside down

It makes it so, an impossibility

That I might be yours,

Eternally

This distance…

How can this be?

So homely

As they pitter patter around

This beauty, bright,

Your smile, immortal

Caressing on my heart

The beautiful distance

Strands silver, skin as worn leather

Yet still, your lips soft as a feather

My hand, forever, holding yours

What distance?

A ballad of fallen angels

Once upon a dead mans dying wish

War waging, a blade to my heart

Friends we once called

I to you – You to I

Then by what calamity brings

You call to our loved ones

A justification, brittle

Crumbling as dust Through your fingers

To my hand

Why, my brother, must we do this dance

History foretells our ending

Thus begins our bow

A performance high as the clouds

"You stole what was mine,"

You breath them

Words, never to ring more true

That day

The day our beloved took her last

"Any hope I had now in a box

Six feet down

Do you know how it felt to watch her die

For no other reason

Than because you lied?"

I feel a tear run down my cheek

His blade butting deeper beneath the skin

A clearer shot I could not take

Yet my finger does not break

This tension throughout my life

bring myself I cannot

To kill the brother I once forgot

For my crime to answer I may

Accept this sentence, here, today

Deeper still the blade doth breach

A grave for two revenge doth seek

I feel the dark waking

My brothers life here for the taking

"I'm sorry,"

I choke as death calling

My last words – Tears falling

We swore to each other, eternal loyalty

Brothers in arms, souls of royalty

Yet here we lie both deserving

What one will take – Both sins

My pistol reserving

Judgment for one

One enough

To reconcile a bond

And never give up

Paper memories

Remember the time

Remember then

That instance,

When, oh when

Our youth, when we did what we did

Didn't care, didn't give

Into the pressures, of parents or peers

Man, those times

Remember?

I do.

I have them all right here

Paper memories in a box

Photographs you might recall

Youth, bliss,

Youth, entertained,

Now we work nine to five

With a mortgage to pay

Remember that time

When we broke in

To Johnny Jimms

And partied till ten

The blues were called

We all got pined

Then the next week we did it again

Paper memories
Of the ones we lost
Of the times we loved
And times forgot

Photographs, I have them all
Photographs, hanging on my wall
Photographs, all of when we wept
Photographs, of the times that left

The house on Poppy Hill

From up on poppy hill

There stands a vacant house, ever still

It watches, we, through bloom lit night

Darkly ominous, shadows in the window,
bright

Who there resides, alive by night?

A family of those long gone

What lives, there, do they live?

Only waking at the rise of the moonlight

Run down, vacant, so it's said

Through all the town's people, so it
spreads

"a ghost and daemon…" the baker shakes

"A murderous, squatter?" the shop owner
quakes

Yet, night by night, I sit in my room

Watching a family from the window bloom

Of the house on poppy hill

Of the house, vacant still

I watch and I wonder, "Whoever could
they be?"

Perhaps they have a child who can come
and play with me

Here at the orphanage, I'm the only one

The one who remains, my bright wishing,
never done

Until the day my family comes

Until then, I'll sit and hum

The song remaining in my head

A song of a family and a bed

A bed by which to call my own

Inside a house, inside a home

Like the one on poppy hill

Ever vacant, ever still

Sneak peak

Here's what's next

A sample excerpt from: Death talks

My upcoming verse novel

Facing death,

Teetering upon the edge of sanity

Blood rushes, pressure builds

Heart pounding,

In this cavity, my sternum

Close… closer now than I've ever been

Mere steps away…

Away from my reckoning

Questions dead,

The answers, very much alive

"Where did you hear that name?"

Excitement trembling off my tongue

Resounding through this vacant street

This man,

Can he even be taken at his word?

Behind his eyes, he's cracking…

The Fight, fighting against something

"Them…"

From his lips the word quivers

"Who?" I press

"Syndicate…

S-S-S-Scorn,

M-Minds,"

With narrowing eyes I ponder

"What about that name?"

My mouth, dry as an Arizona wind

Struggling to speak

"Cavanough…

Mason…"

With every breath he takes,

I see my answers, they're slipping away

Startled, his eyes,

They dart, one point to the next…

Someone is in his head,

A consciousness that shouldn't be

"What is he saying?"

From my lips it pours

The question

A taste,

Sulfur and ash

Burnt beyond repair,

Cinders, what remained of my answers

Now scattered to the winds

The other mind grips the man

Choking his soul,

"He doesn't want these questions asked…"

"Why?" I ask "Why does he care?"

"The Scorn…"

Fear gripping his eyes, he's lost the fight

The pain throbbing, he blinks

"No!"

My tone echoing through the night…

He's gone...

"The Scorn's Affairs,"

That grin, now scarring his face

All the proof that's needed

A puppet… all that's left

The answers,

The truth I've so desperately longed for

Gone… in a blink

"Are none of your concern…"

Slowly creeping, his hand,

Slipping into his jacket

Caution ringing, through every nerve,
Every fiber… of my being

On baited breath I hold,

Unsure of what's to come

Seconds, mere seconds,

No, not even…

Another blink,

Swiftly it touches his chin

The gleam, a cold metal barrel

My eyes wide

Heart racing

Jaw clenched

He doesn't have to do this,

Why?

To make a point?

"Naïve young men,"

His voice vacant and hollow

"Shouldn't stick their noses,"

This faceless man,

This puppeteer,

"Where they don't belong."

Frozen I stand, unable to breath

For fear of pushing him to fire

Cocking it back

Gleaming black of metal

Finger on the trigger hold

One… wrong… move…

It all fades away,

Smoothly, he turns it on me

Honestly, preferable

Better than an innocent,

No knowledge, no choice

"Give up on your answers, boy..."

His tone… venomous

"Or I'll have to bury you,

Like I did them."

In an instant my blood boils

Rage takes hold

Confirmation, I have it

"Who are you?!"

Like Ice, cold and merciless

The words leave me, booming and loud

"I swear,

My tone echoing through the night

"I'm going to end you either way."

"Wrong,"

Hissing like a snake, he grins

"You'll be too dead…"

Answers dead

Questions alive,

Now more powerful,

Louder than even the sound of the gun

"Bang!!!"

If you liked this: you're in for a treat.

In dog eat dog Chicago it's mind over matter

As gangs of psychic youth vi for power.

Yet there's one who has no interest in anything but the truth

The truth of why his father and little sister were murdered.

This quest for answers won't be easy

As silence grip the city

But fortunately Death Talks.

Thank you so much for reading.

If you enjoyed this collection,

Then I've done my job well.

My goal in everything I write, is to make it entertaining

While triggering thought provoking questions

In you, the reader.

If you'd like to support me further

While keeping up to date on my upcoming projects

Follow me on Twitter

@AuthorPDKaiser

Love is the mission statement.

Lets #MakeItEcho

Until tomorrow.

Yours sincerely,

Patrick D. Kaiser

Acknowledgments

This completed work is due

In no small part to my Friend Aaron Smith

Whose vision designed the cover of this book.

Edwina Smith played the role of editor.

And a massive thanks to unsplash.com

For the use of the base photos as the cover.

73